Nature Walk

Maple Trees

by Rebecca Stromstad Glaser

Bullfrog
Books

Ideas for Parents and Teachers

Bullfrog Books let children practice nonfiction reading at the earliest reading levels. Repetition, familiar words, and photo labels support early readers.

Before Reading

- Discuss the cover photo. What does it tell them?
- Look at the picture glossary together. Read and discuss the words.

Read the Book

- "Walk" through the book and look at the photos. Let the child ask questions. Point out the photo labels.
- Read the book to the child, or have him or her read independently.

After Reading

- Prompt the child to think more. Ask: Have you seen a maple tree? How did you know it was a maple?

Bullfrog Books are published by Jump!
5357 Penn Avenue South
Minneapolis, MN 55419
www.jumplibrary.com

Library of Congress Cataloging-in-Publication Data
Glaser, Rebecca Stromstad.
  Maple trees / by Rebecca Stromstad Glaser.
    p. cm. — (Bullfrog books: nature walk)
  Summary: "Describing parts of a maple tree, this photo-illustrated nature walk guide shows very young readers how to identify maple trees. Includes picture glossary"—Provided by publisher.
  Includes bibliographical references and index.
  ISBN 978-1-62031-026-7 (hardcover : alk. paper)
  1. Maple—Juvenile literature. I. Title.
  QK495.A17G53 2013
  583'.78—23   2012009103

Series Editor: Rebecca Glaser
Series Designer: Ellen Huber
Photo Researcher: Heather Dreisbach

Photo Credits: All photos by Shutterstock except: Dreamstime, 5, 7, 10-11, 23br, 23tl; Getty Images, 10; iStockphoto, 1, 22-inset, 24; Veer, 15a, 15b, 23tr

Printed in the United States of America at Corporate Graphics, North Mankato, Minnesota.
7-2012 / 1123
10 9 8 7 6 5 4 3 2

Table of Contents

Looking for Maple Trees

Let's go on a nature walk.
Can you find a maple tree?

Look for a maple leaf.

lobe ·······▶

It has five lobes.

Look for a maple seed.
It has a wing.
Maple seeds spin.

Look for a maple trunk.
A young maple is smooth.
An old maple is rough.

Look for a sap bucket.

Sugar maple sap is
made into syrup. Yum!

13

Look for red, orange, or brown. Maple leaves change color in fall.

Look for bare branches.

In winter, maple
branches are bare.

bud

Look for a bud. It is pointed.
In spring, new leaves will grow.

Have you seen a maple tree?

Parts of a Maple Tree

leaf
A flat, green part of a tree that grows from a branch.

branch
A part of a tree that grows out of its trunk like an arm.

seed
A part of a plant that can grow a new plant.

trunk
The main stem of a tree.

Picture Glossary

bark
The hard outer covering on the outside of a tree.

lobe
Part of a leaf that sticks out from the main part.

bud
A small part of a plant that grows into a leaf or flower.

sap
A liquid that flows through a plant.

Index

To Learn More

Learning more is as easy as 1, 2, 3.

1) Go to www.factsurfer.com

2) Enter "maple trees" into the search box.

3) Click the "Surf" button to see a list of websites.

With factsurfer.com, finding more information is just a click away.